Sherri Thrower
A Sonoma County Foodie

It is my passion to live life creating exciting flavor, serving seasonal dishes and celebrating with outstanding food, great wine, true friends and family. I Love supporti locally owned grocers, farmers and artisan cheese maker

I have been creating custom and gourmet recipe since 1987, and have been very fortunate to live in Sonor County for the last 20 years.

These recipes are simply delicious and I hope you share them with your guests.

Abby's Tuna Melt

6 slices of Danish Gouda
1 Tomato, sliced
10 oz. Albacore Tuna
2 Tb. Yellow Onion, chopped fine
2 Tb. Celery, chopped fine
1 Tb. Parsley, chopped fine
1 Tb. Lemon Juice
1 tsp. Dill
2 Tb. Mayonnaise
1 tsp. Salt
1 tsp. Pepper
4 Slices of Whole Grain (cut on angle)

First drain liquid from the Albacore Tuna. Then mix tuna with mayonnaise, onion, celery, parsley, lemon juice, dill, salt and pepper. Lay out slices of bread. Layer on cheese (3 slices per sandwich) to one side of each sandwich. Then spread tuna mixture over cheese. Finish with tomatoes on top of cheese. Cover. Spread butter on outsides of sandwich. Grill 5-6 minutes. Makes 2 sandwiches. Serve Hot.

The Apple Blossom

4 Slices Swiss Raclette
1 Apple, sliced thin
2 slices of Red Onion
2 Tb. Butter
1 Tb. Sugar
Salt, to taste
Black Pepper, to taste
2 Tb. Pear Chutney
2 Tb. Mayonnaise
4 Slices of Multi Grain Bread

Sauté: Red onions, butter, sugar, salt and pepper. Set aside. Lay out slices of bread. Spread mayonnaise, pear chutney on both sides of each sandwich. Then add cheese, sliced apples, and caramelized onions to one side of each sandwich. Cover. Brush tops of sandwiches with butter. Grill 5-6 minutes. Makes 2 sandwiches. Serve Hot.

Meat Suggestions:
Pancetta,
Honey Turkey

Berry Sweet

Berry Sweet

8 oz. Fromage Blanc
2 Tb. Honey
2 oz. Raspberries
2 oz. Blueberries
1 Tb. Powered Sugar
2 Tb. Butter
4 Slices of Brioche (cut on angle)

Mix cheese with honey, set aside. Lay out slices of bread. Layer cheese mixture on one side of each sandwich. Top cheese with berries. Cover. Spread butter on outsides of sandwich. Grill 2 minutes. Remove and sprinkle powdered sugar over the top. Makes 2 sandwiches. Serve Hot.

Grilled Buttered Rum Banana

4 oz. Whipped Cream Cheese
1 Tb. Honey
2 Bananas, cut length wise
3 Tb. Butter
2 Tb. Dark Rum
2 Tb. Light Brown Sugar
Salt, a touch
1 Tb. Powdered Sugar
4 Slices of Cinnamon Walnut Bread

Mix Cream Cheese with Honey. Spread mixture on both sides of each sandwich. In Sauté pan: Add butter, brown sugar, bananas, and cook for 2 minutes. Then add rum and cook a couple more minutes until liquid has disappeared. Set aside to cool slightly. Apply cooked bananas to one side of each sandwich. Cover. Spread butter to the outside of sandwich. Grill 3 minutes. Sprinkle with powdered sugar. Makes 2 sandwiches. Serve Hot.

<u>Optional</u>: Peanut Butter instead of cream cheese.

The Chantrelle Suprise

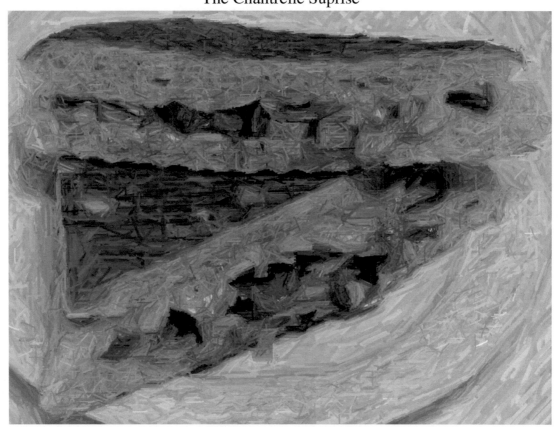

A Chanterelle Surprise

4 Fontina Slices
¼ lb. Grana Padano, shaved
4 Lrg. Chanterelle Mushrooms
1 tsp. Garlic, chopped fine
2 Tb. Butter
Salt, to taste
White Pepper, to taste
1 Leek, cleaned, sliced thin
4 Sage leaves
2 Tb. Mayonnaise
1 Tb. Olive Oil
4 Slices of Focaccia Bread

Heat Sauté Pan with 1 Tb. of butter, add chanterelle mushrooms, garlic, salt, and pepper. Cook a couple of minutes. Set aside. Then Cook leeks with 1 Tb. butter and sage. Cook until soft in texture. Set aside. Lay out bread slices. Spread mayonnaise lightly on both inside halves. Next, layer cheeses and add mushrooms and sautéed leeks. Cover. Lightly brush the outsides with olive oil. Grill 5-6 minutes. Makes 2 sandwiches. Serve Hot.

Cranberry Surprise

⅓ lb. Brie, sliced
14 oz. Can of Whole Cranberries
3 Tb. Brandy
1 Cinnamon Stick
2 oz. Pecans, toasted, chopped
White Pepper, a pinch
1 Tb. Orange Zest
4 Slices of Semolina Cranberry Loaf (cut on angle)

In a saucepan, add cranberries, cinnamon stick, brandy, pecans, orange zest, and white pepper. Cook on medium heat until juice has reduced by half. Set aside to cool. Lay out slices of bread. Layer Brie on one side of each sandwich and then top cheese with the reduced cranberries (about 1 Tb. per sandwich). Cover. Spread butter on outsides of sandwich. Grill 3-4 minutes. Makes 2 sandwiches. Serve Hot.

Meat Suggestion:
Roasted Turkey

Fabulous Fontina

4 oz. Italian Fontina, sliced
½ Red Onion, sliced thin
2 Tb. Butter
1 tsp. Sugar
Salt, to taste
White Pepper, to taste
2 Roma Tomatoes, cut in half
1 Cup Spinach, cleaned, stemmed

1 Bunch Italian Parsley, chopped fine
½ Cup Olive Oil
3 Tb. Lemon Juice
3 Green Onions, sliced thin
3 cloves-Garlic
2 Anchovy filet's
1 Tb. Capers`
4 Slices of Olive Bread (cut on angle)

Roasting tomatoes in oven; seasoned with olive oil, salt and pepper. Cook at 375` for 20 minutes. Set aside to cool. In a sauté pan, cook onions with butter, sugar, salt and pepper until golden. Set aside to cool. To make Pesto: In a bowl add parsley, olive oil, green onions, lemon juice, garlic, anchovies, capers, salt, and black pepper. Mix well then set aside. Lay out slices of bread. Spread pesto on both sides of each sandwich. Then add Fontina cheese to one side of each sandwich. Followed with caramelized onions, roasted tomatoes, and spinach. Cover. Spread butter to the outsides of sandwich. Grill 5-6 minutes. Makes 2 sandwiches. Serve Hot.

Frenchie

6 oz. Fromage d Affinois
4 slices Emmenthaler
2 TB. Dijon Mustard
12 Cornichons, chopped fine or sliced thin
3 TB. Pineapple Marmalade
3 TB. Mayonnaise
2 TB. Butter
4 Slices of Multi Grain Loaf, cut on angle

Lay out slices of bread. Spread to one side of each sandwich the dijon mustard. Mix together mayonnaise and pineapple marmalade and spread over the dijon. Then on the other side, spread the fromage d affinois cheese followed with layers of the Emmenthaler cheese. Sprinkle in the thinly sliced cornichons. Cover. Brush tops of sandwiches with butter. Grill 3-4 minutes. Makes 2 sandwiches. Serve Hot.

Meat Suggestion:
Smoked Ham (sliced thin)

Grilled Cajun Shrimp

4 Slices Fontina d' Aosta
2 Tb. Orange Marmalade
1 tsp. Horseradish
1 tsp. White Wine
White Pepper a dash
1 tsp. Salt
1 Tb. Cajun Spice
2 Tb. Butter
1 Tb. Garlic, chopped fine
8-16-20ct. Prawns, peeled and deveined
1 Tb. Parsley, chopped fine
4 Slices of Semolina Loaf

In Sauté pan: Add 1 Tb. of butter, prawns, cajun spice, cook 3-4 minutes. To make Spread: Mix mayonnaise, orange marmalade, horseradish, white wine, salt and pepper. Spread on both sides of each sandwich. Then on one side of each sandwich, add Caciotta Cascina cheese, then sprinkle parsley on top. Cut prawns length wise and lay on top of cheese. Cover. Spread butter to the outsides of sandwich. Grill 5-6 minutes. Makes 2 sandwiches. Serve Hot.

A Good Choice

4 oz. Boursin Cheese
2 Vine Ripened Tomatoes, sliced
8 Avocado slices
1 Cup Spinach, cleaned, stemmed
2 Tb. Butter
4 Slices of Sourdough

Apply Boursin spread on both sides of each sandwich. Then on one side of each sandwich, layer tomatoes, avocados and spinach. Cover. Spread butter on outsides of sandwich. Grill 5 minutes. Makes 2 sandwiches. Serve Hot.

Meat Suggestion:
Peppered Bacon

The Holy Cow

Holy Cow

3 oz. Whipped Cream Cheese
3 oz. Mountain Gorgonzola
1 Tb. Chives, sliced thin
4 Slices of Vine-Ripened Tomato
6 thin slices of Rare Roast Beef
Salt, to taste
Black Pepper, to taste
1 Tb. Extra Virgin Olive Oil
4 Slices of Garlic Ciabatta

Mix Cream Cheese, Gorgonzola together. Lay out bread slices and spread cream cheese mixture to both sides of each sandwich. Then on one side of each sandwich add the roast beef, tomatoes and season with salt, pepper and chives. Cover. Drizzle extra virgin olive oil over the tops of bread. Grill 2 minutes. Makes 2 sandwiches. Serve Hot.

A Hot & Smokey

8 oz. Smoked Mozzarella, sliced
¼ lb. Sun Dried Tomatoes, drained & sliced
¼ lb. Pesto Sauce
2 Portabella Mushrooms
1 Red Onion, sliced thin
1 Tb. Sugar
Salt, to taste
Black Pepper, to taste
1 cup Arugula, cleaned and trimmed
1 Tb. Extra Virgin Olive Oil
1 Tb. Butter
4 Slices of Sweet French Bread

Grill Portabella Mushrooms with olive oil, salt, and pepper for 5-6 minutes. Set aside to cool. In Sauté pan cook red onions with butter, salt, and sugar until golden. Set aside. Lay out bread slices. Spread pesto to both sides of each sandwich. Next, layer sun dried tomatoes on one side of each sandwich, followed with sliced mozzarella, and topped with the portabella mushrooms, caramelized onions, and arugula. Cover. Grill 5 minutes. Spread butter on outsides of sandwich. Makes 2 sandwiches. Serve Hot.

Jack's Choice

4 oz. Dry Jack (Vella)
1 lg. Heirloom Tomato
2 Tb. Artichoke Jalapeno Dip (Stone mill)
1 Cup Arugula, cleaned
2 Tb. Extra Virgin Olive Oil
Salt, to taste
Black Pepper, to taste
4 slices of Sourdough Bread

Add Artichoke Jalapeño Dip to both sides of the bread, layer both sides of bread with thin slices of dry jack. Add tomatoes, arugula, salt, pepper. Combine. Drizzle extra virgin olive oil over the tops of bread. Grill 5-6 minutes. Makes 2 sandwiches. Serve Hot.

Meat Choices:
Applewood Bacon,
Mild or Hot Italian Sausage

Mama Mia

4 slices Aged Provolone
Cheese
4 oz. Peppered Chevre
4 oz. Chopped Olive Mix
8 oz. Marinated Artichokes,
strained
2 Whole Roasted Red Bell
Peppers, sliced
1 Cup Arugula, packed

4 Tb. Mayonnaise
2 Tb. Basil, julienne
2 Garlic cloves, finely chopped
2 Tb. Parsley, chopped fine
1 Tb. Dijon Mustard
Salt
Black Pepper
4 Slices of Ciabatta Loaf

To make Aioli: Mix mayonnaise, basil, garlic, parsley, dijon, salt and pepper. Set aside. Lay out slices of bread. Spread Aioli on one side of each sandwich. Then on the other side, spread on goat cheese. Followed with the chopped olive mix then roasted peppers, artichokes, arugula, and provolone. Cover. Grill 4-5 minutes. Makes 2 sandwiches. Serve Hot.

Meat Suggestion:
Hot Salami and Smoked Turkey (combined)

The Mediterranean

4 slices Provolone (Grande Brand)
4 slices Mozzarella, whole milk
¼ lb. French Feta (Sheep's Milk)
2 Tb. Mayonnaise
2 Tb. Extra Virgin Olive Oil
4 Tb. Sun Dried Tomatoes, julienne
½ tsp. Red Chili Flakes
4 Tb. Kalamata Olives, pitted and chopped
1 Cup Spinach, cleaned and stemmed
4 Slices of Sourdough Bread

Lay out slices of bread. Spread mayonnaise to both sides of each sandwich, then sprinkle red chili flakes followed with layers of provolone, mozzarella, sun dried tomatoes, feta, kalamata olives, and spinach. Cover. Drizzle olive oil on top of bread. Grill 5-6 minutes. Makes 2 sandwiches. Serve Hot.

A Must Have

¼ lb. Kasserie, sliced
8 Asparagus Stems, trimmed
2 Tb. Red Onion, minced
2 Tb. Italian Parsley, chopped
1 tsp. Mint, chopped fine
4 Slices of Rustic Batard, angled
1 Tb. Dill, chopped fine

¼ lb. Reggiano Parmesan, shaved
3 Tb. Mayonnaise
2 Tb. Olive Oil
½ tsp. Garlic, chopped fine
1 tsp. Dijon Mustard
Salt, to taste
Black Pepper, to taste
1 Tb. Lemon, juiced

To make Herb Aioli: Combine in a bowl, mayonnaise, lemon juice, herbs, garlic, salt, pepper, dijon mustard, and onion. Set aside. Next, roast asparagus with olive oil for 5 minutes and top with salt and pepper. Set aside. Lay out bread slices. Spread Aioli on both sides of each sandwich. Then layer on one side of each sandwich, the asparagus, shaved parmesan, and kasserie. Cover. Lightly brush the outsides with olive oil. Grill 5-6 minutes. Makes 2 sandwiches. Serve Hot.

Meat Suggestions:
Imported Prosciutto,
Mild or Hot Coppa

Redwood Hill

1 Redwood Hill (Crottin), 4 slices
2 Tb. Sesame Seeds
1 Tb. Thyme, chopped fine
1 tsp. Black Pepper
2 Tb. Whole-Grain Mustard
1 Cup Arugula, cleaned
2 Tb. Olive Oil
6 Shitaki Mushrooms, sliced
1 Shallot, sliced thin
2 Tb. Sun-Dried Tomatoes
1 Tb. Garlic, chopped fine
4 Slices of Sourdough Bread

Sprinkle cheese with sesame seeds, thyme, and black pepper. Lay out bread. Spread mustard on both sides of bread. Sauté Mushrooms with olive oil, shallots, garlic, and season with salt and pepper. On one side of each sandwich add cheese, then mushrooms, sun-dried tomatoes, and arugula. Combine. Drizzle extra virgin olive oil over the tops of bread. Grill 5-6 minutes. Makes 2 sandwiches. Serve Hot.

A Savory Apple Treat

4 slices of Wisconsin 3yr. Cheddar
1 Fuji Apple, sliced thin
2 Tb. Apple Butter
2 Tb. Mayonnaise
4 slices of Pumpernickel Bread
1 Tb. Butter

Lay out bread slices. Spread mayonnaise and apple butter on both sides of each sandwich. Then layer cheese and apple slices to one side of each sandwich. Cover. Spread butter on outsides of sandwich. Grill 5-6 minutes. Makes 2 sandwiches. Serve Hot.

Meat Suggestion:
Honey Bacon

Sherri`s "Gold Metal" Winner

4 oz. Abbage de Bel`loc*
2 tsp. Truffle Oil
1 Tb. Extra Virgin Olive Oil
2 Rustic Demi Baguette
4 slices Prosciutto DI Parma

Lay out slices of bread. Drizzle truffle oil on both insides of each sandwich. Add cheese on one side of each sandwich, and then prosciutto. Cover. Brush the outside with extra virgin olive oil. Grill 2-3 minutes. Makes 2 sandwiches. Serve Hot.

* Abbage de Bel'loc: Made with French Pyrenees Sheep's Milk, has a caramelized and rich flavor

Sour Cherry Delight

2 Tb. of Sour Cherry Preserves (Harvest Song)
1 16 oz. Sheep Ricotta
2 Tb. Honey
4 Slices of Brioche Bread (cut on angle)

Mix Ricotta with Honey. Lay out slices of bread. Add ricotta mixture to one side of each sandwich, followed with Sour Cherry Preserve (~1/2 Tb. each sandwich). Combine. Brush tops of sandwiches with butter. Grill 2-3 minutes. Makes 2 sandwiches. Garnish with powdered sugar and rosemary sprig.

Sizzling Cresenza

4 oz. Cresenza (Bellwether Farms)
1 Leek, clean well, slice thin
2 Tb. Butter
½ lb. Bay Shrimp
2 Tb. Mayonnaise
½ Lemon, juiced

1 Tb. Parsley, chopped fine
1 tsp. Old Bay Seasoning
½ tsp. Worcestershire
Salt, to taste
White Pepper, to taste
2 Tb. Olive Oil
4 Slices of Whole Grain Bread

Sauté leeks with butter, salt, and pepper. Set aside. To make shrimp salad: Mix mayonnaise, lemon juice, Old Bay seasoning, worcestershire, salt, white pepper, parsley and shrimp. Top just one side of each sandwich, followed with the cooked leeks. Finish layering with cresenza cheese. Cover. Grill 2-3 minutes. Makes 2 sandwiches. Serve Hot.

Cheese Options:
Havarti with Dill, Monterey Jack,
Whole Milk Mozzarella

A Spanish Flavor

6 oz. Mahon, sliced
6 oz. Peppered Teleme
4 Tb. Olive Spread
2 Tb. Mayonnaise
½ Red Onion, sliced
1 Tb. Sugar
1 Tb. Butter
Salt, to taste
Black Pepper, to taste
4 Slices of Rosemary Focaccia

In a sauté pan, cook onions with butter, sugar, salt and pepper until golden. Set aside. Lay out slices of bread. Spread on one side of each sandwich, mayonnaise, olive spread, teleme, and the caramelized onions. Finish topping with mahon. Cover. Spread butter on outsides of sandwich. Grill 5-6 minutes. Makes 2 sandwiches. Serve Hot.

Meat Suggestion:
Serrano Ham

The Spicy One

4 slices Hot Pepper Jack
4 slices Havarti
2 Tb. Extra Virgin Olive Oil
2 Avocados, sliced
4 oz. Black Olives, sliced
2 Chipotle Peppers in Adobe Sauce
2 Tb. Mayonnaise

1 Vine Ripened Tomato
4 Radishes, sliced thin
1 Roasted Green Chili, diced
Salt, to taste
Black Pepper, to taste
1 Tb. Olive Oil
4 Slices of Garlic Cheddar Bread

Mix mayonnaise with the 'Chipotle peppers & sauce' together. Lay out slices of bread. Spread mayonnaise mixture to both sides of each sandwich. Next layer Jack cheese, avocados, radishes, chilies, olives, and then Havarti cheese. Cover. Brush with Olive Oil. Grill 5-6 minutes. Makes 2 sandwiches. Serve Hot.

Meat Suggestions:
Roasted Pork, Chicken

A Spicy New Yorker

A Spicy New Yorker

4 slices New York (White) Cheddar
6 oz. Southwest Chipotle Pesto
3 Tb. Mayonnaise
1 Sm. Yellow Onion
1 cup Spinach, stemmed and cleaned
6 slices Vine Ripened Tomatoes
8 Jalapeno peppers, sliced and pickled
2 Tb. Butter
4 Slices of Sun Dried Tomato Focaccia Bread

Sauté onions with 1 Tb. of butter, salt and pepper. Set aside. Mix mayonnaise with pesto together and spread to both sides of each sandwich. Then layer on one side of each sandwich, layer the cheddar, onions, spinach, tomatoes, and jalapeno's. Cover. Grill 5-6 minutes. Makes 2 sandwiches. Serve Hot.

Meat Suggestions:
Grilled Chicken,
Tri Tip,
Pulled Pork

Sweet Blues

4 oz. Stilton Blue Cheese, sliced
1 Pear, sliced
2 Tb. Honey
2 Tb. Butter
1 Cup Spring Mix (salad greens)
2 Tb. Almonds, sliced and toasted
4 Slices of Sourdough Walnut Bread

Lay out slices of bread. Layer on to one side of each sandwich the honey, butter, blue cheese slices, sliced pear, toasted almonds, and spring mix. Cover. Grill 5-6 minutes. Serve Hot. Makes 2 sandwiches.

A Sweet Italian Treat

4 oz. Plin di Capra
2 Tb. Pear Chutney
3 Pears, peeled and diced
3 Tb. Golden Raisins
½ cup Sugar
1 cups Water
1 cup Apple Juice-Fresh
1 Tb. Apple Cider Vinegar

4 Peppadew Peppers, chopped
1 Tb. Lemon Juice
2 Cloves
Pinch of all spice
1 Cinnamon Stick
Pinch of salt
Pinch of white pepper
4 Slices of Sourdough Walnut Bread

In a stockpot, add in all ingredients (except cheese). Bring "chutney" to a boil then turn down heat and let simmer for 20 minutes. Set aside to cool and thicken. Layer your plin di capra (cheese) to one side of each slice of each sandwich, followed with the "thickened" Chutney heavily. Cover. Grill 3 minutes. Makes 2 sandwiches. Serve Hot.

   * Plin di Capra: A soft, mild rind, goats milk with a touch of cows cream added

Taylor's Favorite

Taylor's Favorite

6 slices Whole Milk Mozzarella
4 slices Provolone
¼ lb. Asiago, shredded
4 Tomato slices
6 Mushrooms-Cremini
3 oz. Green Olives, sliced
½ Yellow Bell Pepper, thin slices

2 Tb. Red Onion, chopped fine
2 Tb. Basil, fresh
1 tsp. Oregano, chopped fine
1 Tb. Garlic, chopped fine
2 Tb. Butter
1 Tb. Olive Oil
4 Slices of Rosemary Ciabatta

In pan, sauté with 1 Tb. butter the sliced cremini mushrooms and garlic. Season with salt and pepper. Cook a few minutes or until golden in color and soft. Set aside. On one side of each sandwich, layer mozzarella, asiago, all of the vegetables then top with provolone. Cover. Grill 5-6 minutes. Makes 2 sandwiches. Serve Hot.

Meat Suggestions:
Pepperoni,
Fennel Salami,
Hot Salami,
Meatloaf

The Vineyard

4 oz. Taleggio Cheese
¼ lb. Red Seedless Grapes cut in half
2 Tb. Olive Oil
Salt, to taste
Black Pepper, to taste
4 Slices of Country Walnut Bread, cut on angle

Spread Taleggio on each side of both sandwiches. Layer grapes on one side of each sandwich. Season with salt and pepper. Cover. Drizzle Olive Oil. Grill 3 minutes. Makes 2 sandwiches. Serve Hot.

Open Face Sandwich

Cranberry Blue Cheese Bruschetta

½ cup Cranberry Sauce, wholeberries
1 Tb. Orange Zest
2 Tb. Brandy
½ tsp. Salt
White Pepper, to taste
½ tsp. Cinnamon
Mix ingredients in bowl, Set aside.
6 oz. Bleu d'Auvergne
6 slices Whole Grain with Walnuts, sliced and toasted

To Assemble
Add cranberry mixture to toasted bread, top with blue cheese, broil until melted.

Gorgonzola, Pear & Honey

¼ cup Ex-virgin Olive Oil
6 oz. Imported Gorgonzola
3 Tb. Honey
4 slices Dried Pears, chopped fine
1 Sweet Baguette, sliced into 12 slices

Cooking Instructions

Pre heat the oven to 400'. Arrange the sliced baguettes on a baking sheet. Brush with olive oil. Bake until the bread is lightly golden and crisp about 8 minutes. Arrange the cheese and dried fruit on top of toasts and bake until the cheese is melted, about 3 minutes. Drizzle toast with honey. Eat right away!

Mediterranean Bruschetta

¼ cup Olive Oil
3 ½ cup Eggplant, unpeeled, small dice
¾ cup Onion, chopped fine
¼ cup Celery, finely chopped
½ cup Green "pitted" Olives, chopped fine
3 Tb. Capers, drained and chopped
¼ cup Red Wine Vinegar

2 Tb. Sugar
3 Tb. Golden Raisins
3 Tb. Pinenuts, toasted
1 cup Roma Tomatoes, small dice
¼ cup Italian Parsley, chopped fine
6 slices of Ciabatta

Cooking Instructions

In Skillet, heat 2 Tb. of Olive Oil over medium heat. Cook eggplant, stirring for 3-5 minutes, or until tender, and transfer to bowl. Add to skillet the remaining olive oil and cook onion, celery cook 5 minutes.

Add Olives, capers, vinegar, sugar, raisins, tomato and the Pinenuts, cover, cook 6-8 minutes or until celery is tender. Transfer to bowl, cool. Before serving add parsley.

Cheese Choices

Caciocavallo Aged Provolone,
Tallegio,
Ewephoria Gouda

Add cheese (Sliced or grated) to bread, toast until cheese is melted and add 1 Tb. "Bruschetta" to tops.

South West Chili Chevre

1– 4oz. Redwood Hill Chili Chevre
½ Avocado, finely chopped
1 Vine-Ripened Tomato, remove seeds, finely chop
½ bunch Cilantro, rough chop
6 Garlic Bread, slices

Slice bread, add goat cheese, avocado, tomato, and cilantro. Good either toasted or cold!

White Bean, Swiss Chard Bruschetta

¼ lb. Pancetta, cubed
3 cloves Garlic, chopped fine
1 cup Cannelloni Beans, drained
2 Tb. Ex-Virgin Olive Oil
½ tsp. Red Chili Flakes
10 Basil leaves, sliced thin
1/2 cup Diced Tomatoes, Drained
2 Tb. Oregano, chopped fine
2 cups Swiss Chard, cleaned and chopped
1 cup Chicken Broth

Cooking Instructions
Cook pancetta in 1 Tb. olive oil. until golden brown. Set aside. With 2 cups Swiss
Chard, boil 10 minutes in chicken broth; Drain. Add all ingredients together.
Cheese Choices
Bellwether Papato, Ricotta Salata Teleme

Cream Cheese Spreads

Crostini

1 Loaf French Bread
¼ tsp. Salt
¼ tsp. Ground Black Pepper
Extra Virgin Olive Oil

Cooking Instructions

Pre heat the oven to 400*F. Trim the ends off of the bread and cut crosswise into ¼-inch thick slices. Arrange the slices on a baking sheet. Brush with olive oil (both sides). Bake for about 6 minutes, until the bread is lightly golden and crisp (turning the baking sheet around midway may help even browning). Cool crostini completely before serving. Makes about 30+ crostini.

Artichoke Spread

1– 8oz. Whipped Cream Cheese
2 Tb. Milk
1– 14oz. Artichokes in water
1 Tb. Lemon Juice
1 tsp. Lemon Zest
1 Tb. Jalapeno Pepper
2 Tb. Asiago, shredded
1 Tb. Elephant Garlic

Add all ingredients to the food processor. Blend well.

Blue Cheese Spread

1- 8oz. Whipped Cream Cheese
2 Tb. Milk
¼ cup Imported Gorgonzola
2 Tb. Parsley
¼ cup of Red Apples
Optional- your favorite nut

Add all ingredients to the food processor. Blend well.

Chipotle Cream Spread

1– 8oz. Whipped Cream Cheese
2 Tb. Milk
2 Chipotle Peppers with adobe sauce
1 Tb. Lime Juice
1 Tb. Garlic
1 Tb. Cilantro

Add all ingredients to the food processor. Blend well.

Chocolate Strawberry Spread

1– 8oz. Whipped Cream Cheese
2 Tb. Milk
4 Tb. Ricotta
3 Tb. Maple Syrup
2 Tb. Sliced Almonds, toasted
1 tsp. Kahlua
Blend the above in food processor, then add:
6 Lrg. Strawberries, chopped
4 Tb. Chocolate Chips

Add all ingredients to the food processor. Blend well.

Classic Pesto Spread

1 bunch Basil, stems removed, leaves only
½ cup Parsley
½ cup shredded Parmesan
2 Tb. Pinenuts or Walnuts
5 cloves Garlic, peeled
2/3 cup Olive Oil
Kosher Salt
Black Pepper

Add to food processor the first five ingredients. Blend well. While food processor is running, add olive oil until it is completely combined (a couple of minutes).

Cream Cheese, Cheddar & Roasted Pepper Spread

8oz. Whipped Cream Cheese
2 Tb. Milk
1 ½ cups Sharp Cheddar
½ cup Roasted Yellow Peppers
2 tsp. Dijon Mustard
1 tsp. Paprika
2 Tb. Green Onion

Add all ingredients to the food processor. Blend well.

EggPlant Spread

1- 8oz. Whipped Cream Cheese
2 Tb. Milk
½ Eggplant, peeled and roasted
1 Tb. White Garlic, roasted
5 large leaves Basil
Kosher Salt
Black Pepper

Add all ingredients to the food processor. Blend well.

Herb Cream Cheese Spread

1– 8oz. Whipped Cream Cheese
2 Tb. Milk
1 tsp. Dijon Mustard
2 tsp. Garlic
1 Tb. Parsley
1 Tb. Chives
1 tsp. Basil

Add all ingredients to the food processor. Blend well.

Olive and Rosemary Spread

8oz. Whipped Cream Cheese
2 Tb. Milk
2 Tb. Green Olives, pitted
2 Tb. Black Olives, pitted
 2 Tb. White Garlic
1 Tb. Rosemary
1 Tb. Parsley
1 Tb. Roasted Red Pepper
1 Tb. Caperberries

Add all ingredients to the food processor. Blend well.

Parsley Pesto Spread

1 bunch Italian Parsley
3 Green Onions, rough chop
3 Tb. Lemon Juice
3 cloves Garlic
2 Anchovy Filets
1 Tb. Capers
¼ cup Ex-Virgin Olive Oil
Kosher Salt
Black Pepper

Add to food processor the first six ingredients. Blend well. While food processor is running, add olive oil until it is completely combined (a couple of minutes).

Peppered Goat Cheese Spread

1- 8oz. Whipped Cream Cheese
2 Tb. Milk
4 oz. Redwood Hill Peppered Chevre
1 tsp. White Garlic
1 Tb. Chives
1 tsp. Lemon Thyme

Add all ingredients to the food processor. Blend well.

Spinach Pesto Spread

2 bunch of Spinach cleaned and cooked. Squeeze out liquid
1 cup Parsley, stems removed
3 cloves Garlic, peeled
2 Tb. Lemon Juice
2 Tb. Pecorino Romano, shredded
2/3 cup Ex-Virgin Olive Oil
Black Pepper, to taste

**Add to food processor the first five ingredients. Blend well. While food processor
is running, add olive oil until it is completely combined (a couple of minutes).**

Sun Dried Tomato Spread

1– 8oz. Whipped Cream Cheese
2 Tb. Milk
8 oz. Sun Dried Tomatoes, strain
1 Tb. Oregano
2 Tb. Kalamata Olives
1 Tb. White Garlic
2 Tb. Sheep Feta, crumbled

Add all ingredients to the food processor. Blend well.

Sweet Nut Spread

1 – 8oz. Whipped Cream Cheese
2 Tb. Milk
¼ cup Toasted Walnuts or Pecans
2 Tb. Honey or Light Brown Sugar
Optional: Dried Fruits, Fresh fruit or Preserves

Add all ingredients to the food processor. Blend well.

Wild Mushroom Spread

1- 8oz. Whipped Cream Cheese
2 Tb. Milk
1 Tb. Thyme leaves
1 tsp. Dijon
1 tsp. Elephant Garlic
Kosher Salt
*8 oz. Assorted Mushrooms, cleaned and sliced
*1 Shallot
*1 Tb. Butter

First Sauté sliced mushrooms and shallots with 1 Tb. of butter. Cool before adding rest of ingredients to the food processor. Blend well.

Sandwich Tips

Use Brick for weight, Panini Press, Waffle Iron or Cast Iron Weight.

The Sharper the Cheese the Better!

Try Compound Butters using Garlic, Herbs and Chutney's.

Cream Cheese Spreads.

Add Herbs to your Mayonnaise for unique flavors.

Add Preserves to your Mayonnaise for amazing taste.

Mustards are a great addition to any sandwich.

Cheese Tips

BUYING: Don't buy "on-sale", it's probably past its date. Buy only the amount
you can use in a week or so. Check sell-by dates.

SERVING: Sliced for sandwiches; Chunked, wedged and/or sliced for cheeseboard;
Melted for a sauce; Grated as a garnish.

STORING: Refrigerate all unused cheese. Cheese must breathe to stay vibrant.
Plastic touching the cheese may cause it to sweat and slime. Discard store wrapper
(or keep with cheese for identification).
Rewrap in wax paper.
Store in vegetable bin (set at high humidity).
Shred cooking cheese prior to refrigeration or freezing.
Bleu cheese mold may spread everywhere. Sanitize area and wrap well.

GRATING: Fine Grater for hard cheese; Coarse grater for semi-hard. Best to grate only
when needed. Wrap excess in wax paper then refrigerate. Add a teaspoon or
so of cornstarch, shake then freeze in zipper bag. Parmigiano and Romano freeze
well. Softer cheeses grate more easily when in freezer for 30 min.

HEATING: Cheese melts best when a hot liquid is already present. Melt 1 Tb.
butter over med. heat, stir in 1 Tb. flour, add 1 cup milk, stir to thicken, add 1-2
cups shredded cheese, stir to combine and melt.

Types of Cheese

FRESH –RINDLESS (SOFT UNRIPENED) 45%-85%: Examples are Cottage, Cream, Ricotta, and Panir; And Short-cured cheeses such as Feta.

HARD: The most demanding of cheese processes, curds destined for a hard cheese must go through multiple cutting, heating, layering, and pressing steps before it develops it unique traits; Examples are Cheddar, Parmigiano, Romano and Swiss varieties.

NATURAL RIND: Goat milk based. This blue-gray rind type is most commonly found in French country cheeses; Examples are Chevr'e.

COOKED & KNEADED: Provolone and Mozzarella.

SOFT-RIPENED: Cured from the outside in. These are treated with a penicillium mold, creating a bloomy type of rind; Examples are Brie and Camembert.

SEMI-HARD(45%): Some of the whey is replaced with water, contributing to a "washed curd" process; May be classified as Gouda-Style; Most are wrapped in wax; Example Gouda and Edam.

SEMI-SOFT: Generally rindless and soft textured. Common for sandwiches or cheeseboards; Examples are Fontina, Havarti, Jack and Colby.

WASHED-RIND: Cheese left to ripen on its own tends to form a gray, bitter rind. Periodic washing causes a favorable bacterial reaction, creating the distinctive coating characteristic of certain cheeses. Common washes are beer, wine, brandy, brine, whey or oil.

Pairing Cheese with Wine

<u>GENERAL RULE</u>: Full-bodied cheese (**Emmental, Cheddar, Gouda**) goes well with full-bodied wine (Merlot, Beaujolais). Light sweet cheese (**Brie, Camembert**) with (Sparkling Rose, Champagne, Pinot Noir).

<u>AROMATIC VARIETIES</u>: (**Blue, Limburger**) complements a strong red wine or a heavy (Burgundy, Shiraz, Sauvignon). A contrast is achieved by pairing them with a (Port or Sherry).

<u>MEDIAN VARIETIES</u>: Milder cheese (**Edam, Gouda, Cheddar**) compliments a milder wine (Pinot Gris, Pinot Noir, Chardonnay).

<u>MILK VARIETIES</u>: **Sheep's milk** cheese pairs well with fruity or sweet wine such as (Gewürztraminer, Sauternes). **Goat cheese** works with whites, like (Sauvignon Blanc, Pinot Gris, Riesling)

Basic Green "Side" Salad

2 cups Baby Green Lettuce
½ cup Grape Cherry Tomatoes
2 Tb. Italian Parsley, chopped fine

Dressing:
2 Tb. VerJus (Terra Sonoma)
2 Tb. Extra Virgin Olive Oil
1 tsp. Shallot, chopped fine
1 tsp. Honey
Sea Salt
Fresh Cracked Black Pepper

Optional:
Berries or Apples
Caramelized Nuts
Cheese

Classic Tomato Soup

2 ½ lb. Vine Ripened Tomatoes
6 cloves Garlic, peeled
2 small Yellow Onions, sliced
½ cup Ex-virgin Olive Oil
1 qt. Chicken Broth
2 Bay Leaves
4 Tb. Butter
¾ cup Heavy Cream
½ cup Basil
Preheat oven to 450`

Roast Tomatoes on a baking sheet with garlic and onions drizzle with olive oil until everything is coated. Season with Salt and Pepper. Roast for 30 minutes until golden in color.

Add ingredients to stockpot with chicken broth, butter and bay leaves. Bring to a boil. Reduce heat and cook 20-30 minutes more. Liquid should reduce by a third. Remove Bay leaves. Next, add basil leaves to pot. Use a hand blender to blend tomato mixture until smooth texture. Slowly add cream and season with salt and pepper! Enjoy this fabulous soup!